CW00871577

CONTENTS

As described on the opposite page, the publishers of this book are concerned to protect the rights of the writers and owners of these songs, while making it simple for people to use the songs widely in Christian ministry. Accordingly this contents page is laid out so that you can mark it as an aid to record keeping and in the spirit of the copyright arrangement. Just tick the song when you have made an overhead projection transparency or flash-card copy.

HAVE YOU HEARD OF THE TRIM TEST?
How to choose suitable songs for gospelling.

This simple test shows you how to select Christian songs which will be effective in evangelistic and outreach programs.

Does the song **TEACH** what is true and worthy?
Are Bible stories and biblical teaching handled well?
Is there any material which children will have to unlearn as they grow?
Is God treated with reverence?
Are people treated with respect?
Is the gospel of God's grace clearly presented?

Are the words **RELATED TO LIFE**? Do they relate to the world of today and the world of the child?
Is any presumptive language used? These are words which the children are invited to sing which may be outside their experience. This is specially sensitive outreach contexts. Songs which may be suitable for church services and which use language of commitment are not appropriate for an open crowd at an outreach event or an open classroom.

Is the song **INTERESTING**? Are the lyrics, rhythm, style and tune enjoyable? Does the program offer a range of musical styles including rock, ballads, swing, blues etc.? Are the words memorable?

Do the words **MAKE SENSE** to children?
Is the language contemporary? Are the grammar and phrasing straightforward?
Are the biblical quotations from a modern translation?

THEMES AND TEACHING SUGGESTIONS

No one is suggesting that every occasion for singing should be a time for lengthy explanations, however there will be times when an apt song is needed to support the theme of a teaching or gospelling program. These teaching suggestions are brief notes which may suggest biblical ideas and stories with some tips for introducing the song and a guide to suitability.

All day long
Suitable for 7+ age-group. Supports the idea of God's constant love. Just as we can't stop the sun rising and setting, people being born and dying, so we can't stop God from loving us!

The blind man
Suitable for 10+ age-group. Theme: Jesus is the way to God (John 14.6) Be aware that some children will think literally about 'the way to go home'. A very brief clue will help them to make the link to the good news that Jesus is the way to a wonderfully close relationship with God.

The boom boom song
Suitable for 9+ age-group. This light and jaunty song will support teaching about the death and resurrection of Jesus.

Can you count the stars?
Suitable for 7+ age-group. This song connects the idea of God as powerful creator with Jesus, his Son our friend. Psalm 8.

The caterpillar song
Suitable for 7+ age-group. Use, if possible, a live caterpillar, a chrysalis and a butterfly (or show pictures) to show the change that happens. Use this song to support the story of Easter and show the great joy of the resurrection news. John 11.25-26; 14.18-20, 1 Corinthians 15.3-6.

Choosing Jesus
Suitable for 9+ age-group. This song supports the idea that Jesus welcomes seemingly unlikely people and that following him means a new way of living. Luke 5.31,32; Philippians 4.8-9; 2 Corinthians 5.17-18.

Don't let the devil take the truth away
Suitable for 10+ age-group. This song was written to reinforce the teaching of Jesus in his parable of the sower, the soil and the seed in Matthew 13. It shows how easy it is to be distracted from allowing the teaching of Jesus to grow in our lives.

Driftin' away
Suitable for 9+ age-group. Gospelling involves helping people to see the reality of sin and evil. Many children's workers show sin as a catalogue of 'naughty things we do'. This song takes a different approach: it shows the main problem as broken relationships between people and between us and God. Luke 15.11-32; Romans 5.10-11; 2 Coninthians 5.20. Jesus never turns anyone away: John 6.37. He is the one who can really put wrecked things together again.

Footsteps
Suitable for 10+ age-group. Encourage the children to imagine the footsteps of Jesus going everywhere inviting, welcoming, calling. Mark 6.34; Matthew 4.18-22. Encourage them to further imagine Jesus not just in Israel *then*, but in our locality *now*, still inviting, welcoming, calling.

Get up!

Suitable for 6+ age-group. A bouncy, positive song to encourage gratitude for each new day and to encourage children to see each day as an opportunity to live with Jesus.

Actions: Get up out of bed *(Crouch down and spring up)* Have a yawn *(Hand over mouth)* Scratch you head *(Scratch)* And say 'Thank you' *(Lift left palm upwards)* It's a brand new day *(Lift both palms upwards)* Stretch out *(Arms outstretched sideways)* touch your toes *(Bend over and touch your toes)* Blink *(Clench eyes and fists)* your eyes and *(Open eyes wide and stretch hands)* blow your nose *(Hand to nose)* And say 'Thank you' etc *(As above)*.

Give thanks to the Lord

Suitable for 5+ age-group. An energetic song, especially if you invent your own actions. Even if you don't you are likely to run out of breath (there are no breaks between the verses!) but this adds to its charm as it leads us to be thankful to God right through the day in the words of Psalms 107 and 118.

God is love

Suitable for 11+ age-group. A gentle round celebrating God's love. John 3.16; 15.13; 1 John 4.19.

God loves you just the way you are

Suitable for 6+ age-group. The advertisers tell us that we are attractive and loveable when we wear this or look like that or buy the other. God's message to us is in direct contrast to this propaganda. Isaiah 44.24.

God made caterpillars

Suitable for 5+ age-group. A delightful song in the spirit of Psalm 8 connecting God's powerful creativity and his quest for a personal relationship with us.

God made the world

Suitable for 5+ age-group. Design your own actions and enjoy singing about God the Creator. Links with the Genesis 1 story and Psalm 104.

God with a loving heart

Suitable for 7+ age-group. Another song with the strong, classic theme that the great Creator of all the universes has a personal and caring love for us all.

Good Fri, Good Fri, Good Friday

Suitable for 10+ age-group. A supporting song for an exploration of the story of Jesus' death, at Easter or any other time of the year. Use the Matthew 27 account to link with the episodes mentioned in this song.

He gets things done

Suitable for 10+ age-group. A gentle, thoughtful ballad which will repay exploration. It shows another facet of God's style which is different from the 'mighty strong' image in a couple of other songs in this collection. Biblical themes in this mood include the 'quiet' conversion of Lydia (Acts 16.14-15), the 'quiet' miracles (Luke 5.12-16) and the temptation to Jesus to conquer the world in showy power (Matthew 4.1-11) Make sure the children understand the references to Jesus' birth and death in the third verse. Mark 4.26-29.

The helping song

Suitable for 7+ age-group. Begin with the chorus, then add the verses as you introduce the stories from the Gospels which are mentioned. Zacchaeus (Luke 19.1-10), Bartimaeus (Mark 10.46-52) Mary and Martha (Luke 10.38-42) and the woman who gate-crashed Simon's dinner party (Luke 7.36-39).

How much am I worth?

Suitable for 10+ age-group. This is another song with a theme worth exploring over a period. You can begin with the first verse and the chorus only. Then enriched with your teaching program or through little drama sketches, you can add the other verses. Verse 2 (Matthew 10.29-31), verse 3 (Luke 15.8-10), verse 4 (Luke 15.1-7, 11-24), verse 5 (Romans 5.6-8).

If you're black or if you're white

Suitable for 7+ age-group. A fun way to reinforce the theme that God's gracious love is offered to all and is totally undeserved. Can be very enjoyable sung in old Al Jolson style. Could be connected to the story of Zacchaeus (Luke 19.1-10) or the king in Jesus' parable of the unmerciful servant (Matthew 18.23-35) or Jesus' teaching that God's indiscriminate love is showered on all (Matthew 5.43-45).

I have a name

Suitable for 6+ age-group. Children's workers work hard to make sure they remember and use the children's names: in this way they express the nature of God who knows us intimately. The children can do their part towards making their part of the world more friendly and liveable. The Gospels are rich with accounts of Jesus demonstrating this kind of personal love and care. To see him was to see God's parental and personal concern. John 1.47-51; 14.8-11; Mark 10.14-16; Psalm 121.

Image of God

Suitable for 11+ age-group. The creation story in Genesis 1.26-27 is the source of this idea. Ask the children whether anyone has ever remarked that they remind people of other members of their family ... 'chip off the old block', 'like father, like son/like mother, like daughter'. It may be suggested by looks or mannerisms or facial expressions. God made us with a number of special characteristics, not as the animals wonderful as they are. Such aspects of our nature remind us of God's nature ... choosing, creating, seeing right from wrong, communicating, thinking. Some children may find the connections in the verses of this song difficult to jump conceptually: if so, forget the verses and just use the chorus by itself.

I need a friend

Suitable for 7+ age-group. Everyone goes through bad days. Children know that having good friends makes all the difference during the tough times. Jesus is the best friend ever. It is important that we don't teach that knowing Jesus has some kind of magic to bring good luck in all circumstances. In fact, knowing Jesus can sometimes make life tougher! Matthew 14.22-33. John 11 contains the moving evidence of Jesus' warm friendship with the Bethany family.

It's an adventure

Suitable for 10+ age-group. The themes in this little song lend themselves to use in an ongoing program where there is some contact with children over a period. The first followers of Jesus certainly discovered an element of adventure just being with him. Our programs need to be marked with that spirit, otherwise we can be accused of promoting a blandness which doesn't belong in Jesus' kingdom.

I've never seen an elephant

Suitable for 7+ age-group. Many children love animal fun songs. This one reinforces the idea that we are special. God has made us as individuals.

Jesus came
Suitable for 9+ age-group. Like *I have a name* this song reinforces the idea that Jesus demonstrated in his life on earth the kind of compassion and loyalty which is part of God's essential nature. This song is best used in a teaching program which draws on the Gospels for stories of Jesus with people, such as the story of the Samaritan woman (John 4) or Jesus' willingness to break social convention in the healing of people with leprosy.

Jesus is greater
Suitable for 10+ age-group. Most children have heroes - celluloid heroes and rock stars, sporting heroes, even older friends. Jesus can be a hero because he is powerful, because he is a close friend and because he gave his life for us. John 14.6; 15.13; Luke 8.22-25 and 9.28-36.

Jesus is the best friend
Suitable for 4+ age-group. The disarmingly simple message is well suited for younger children. Mark 10.13-16

Jesus loves the boys and girls
Suitable for 4+ age-group. Like *Jesus is the best friend*, this song uses Mark 1.13-16 as its theme.

Light of the world
Suitable for 9+ age-group. To prevent the idea of Jesus as 'Light' being lost to the children because it is abstract, leaders should talk personally about how following the teaching of Jesus makes sense in the reality of their lives. Jesus used this picture of himself in the story of the blind man in John 9. See also John 8.12.

Mighty God
Suitable for 9+ age-group. Boys particularly will appreciate this song with its 'macho' style. It is a neat counterpoint to the quieter *He gets things done*. Both themes give us a rounded picture of God's nature. Note the contrast between the fiction characters (Superman and King Kong) and the reality of God. The strongest thing God does is to deal with sin and evil, both in our lives and further afield. The death and resurrection of Jesus is the ultimate act of strength!
Try the actions: He's a mighty God *(Strongman stance, fists and arms)* and he's mighty strong *(Bodybuilder stance, fists and arms above)* He can change the world *(Arms in wide circular motion ending up across the body)* even beat King Kong *(Beat breast like gorilla)* And he cares for us *(Hug yourself)* in so many ways *(Reach out widely)* If we trust in him *(Arms aloft, hands open)* we will grow and change *(Hands together as if praying, then upward and back to sides in a circular motion)*. Stronger than any man *(Squat relaxed then rise slowly and adopt strongman stance)* Bad guys run and hide *(Arms covering face as if in fear)* He's on our side! *(Punch the air with both hands one after the other)*

Millions of people
Suitable for 10+ age-group. Children like to be inspired by dreams of a better world either on a global scale or in their own circumstances. They often have a fine sense of fairness. However they also know about the realities in the world. This song connects those realities with the other great reality - the love of God.

Mystery world
Suitable for 11+ age-group. A song which invites older children to explore the big questions like the state of the world and the coming of Christ into it all. This song does not explain the questions or offer clear answers; it just invites children to consider that Jesus can offer possibilities beyond our imagination.

No mountain high enough
Suitable for 10+ age-group. Another song which reinforces the teaching that God's grace and love are unconquerable: in the end there is nothing in my world that cuts out the possibility of God's being available to me. Based on Romans 8.35-39.

123 Follow me
Suitable for 7+ age-group. This song connects Jesus' calling of his disciples with the call to people today to follow him similarly. Luke 5.1-11; 9.18-25; 10.38-42; 18.28-34.

Only Jesus
Suitable for 7+ age-group. With a touch of humour, this song shows that Jesus is the only one to open up the way to heaven to a forever relationship with God. John 14.1-7; Romans 6.23; Luke 14.15-24.

Our God is so big
Suitable for 7+ age-group. All children love to sing this, but boys enjoy it better than many other Christian songs. This is probably because God is shown to be strong, active and energetic. Such a song can be teamed with stories of some of the Bible heroes of faith. People like Paul and Silas (Acts 16.16-40), Elijah (1 Kings 18), Daniel and co. (Daniel 3 and 6)

Younger children would enjoy some actions: Our God is so big *(One arm punch with clenched fist)* so strong and so mighty *(Other arm punching too),* there's nothing our God cannot do *(arms lowered waving horizontally, palms down).* The mountains are his *(Signal high peak)* the rivers are his *(hands show running water descending)* the whole world *(arms trace large circle)* is under his smile *(trace very large grin).*

Road sign song
Suitable for 7+ age-group. This song can be introduced by preparing a set of road signs on cardboard ... STOP, ONE WAY, WRONG WAY GO BACK, NO THROUGH ROAD, GIVE WAY. To these can be added a signpost pointing in opposite directions ... MY WAY and GOD'S WAY. Joshua 24.15; Matthew 7.13-14; John 6.66-69; 14.6.

Sandy Lands
Suitable for 9+ age-group. Jesus' parable of the two builders in Matthew 7.24-29 graphically shows the good sense of taking notice of what he says and the way he tells us to live. *Sandy Lands* is a fine support for the telling of that story.

See the little seed
Suitable for 5+ age-group. A song to celebrate growing and life. Actions can easily be added by becoming very small on the ground then 'growing' in the last line. In verse 2, the boys start small while the girls point; in verse 3 change places. Jesus too started very small and grew, learning to please his parents and God his Father (Luke 2.39-40).

Sorrowing Song
Suitable for 10+ age-group. Many songs for children are happy and bouncy. This song suggests a wondering mood: introduce it as a quieter thinking song. Connect the evil we see around us with the wrong things in our own lives. And not just the wrong things we have

done, but the wrong things that have been done to us. Some of the children in your group will have experienced terrible and fearful things. Jesus is involved with helpless and hurting people in today's world. Luke 19.41-44; Psalm 2.1-3.

Special
Suitable for 7+ age-group. Invite the children to bring to mind their experiences of other kids teasing them for their looks or the things they have. Show them that God certainly does not take advantage of people in this way. His love does not discriminate; unfailingly constant. Proverbs 17.5

Stop still and listen
Suitable for 7+ age-group. Like several others in this collection, this song helps us to celebrate the powerful creativity of God and his personal care and interest in us. Use the sound effects for extra fun and interest.

Thank you for the friends
Suitable for 5+ age-group. A set of colourful pictures to illustrate this song would help younger children think about the words of this song.

This is God's world
Suitable for 7+ age-group. Children are increasingly conscious of the need to look after our world and our neighbourhood. Here we remind the children that this is not just our world or their world - but God's world. Gospelling can include enlisting children for a cause of concern to God. Genesis 1.26-28; Psalm 8.6-8; Romans 8.19-22.

Together
Suitable for 5+ age-group. This is a rallying song for use in an ongoing program where a positive group spirit is possible.

Where do all the good things come from?
Suitable for 7+ age-group. Building on a child's fascination for interesting and unusual things, this song shows two aspects of God's creativity - making things and re-making things.

Wider than the universe
Suitable for 5+ age-group and across a wide span. A celebration of God's love. Could be accompanied on occasion by someone talking personally and briefly about how he/she has experienced God's love.

Yes, God is bigger than I am
Suitable for 10+ age-group. Like others in this book, here we have the connection between God's great power and his caring attentiveness to our needs.

How to make your OHP transparency without copying the spiral wire!
Cut a strip of white paper about 15 mm wide and 300 mm long. Lay this strip on the copier glass against the leading edge. Then place *Gospelling to the Beat* on the glass with the spiral sitting on the paper strip. Close the lid and copy!

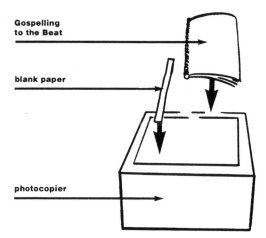

Gospelling to the Beat

blank paper

photocopier

All Day Long

Words and music: Paul Field

Liltingly.

2. The tide rolls out and the tide rolls in, all day long.
Lives are ending and lives begin, all day long.
God keeps loving us all of the time,
His love never gives in.

9

ALL DAY LONG

The sun comes up and the sun goes down,
all day long -
The world keeps turning around and round,
all day long -
People keep waking up, people asleep,
God is loving them all.

CHORUS
All day long, all day long -
God's love goes on and on.

The tide rolls out and the tide rolls in,
all day long.
Lives are ending and lives begin,
all day long.
God keeps loving us all of the time,
His love never gives in.

Words and music: Paul Field
© 1991 Daybreak Music Ltd

The Blind Man

Words and music: Anonymous
This arrangement (C) 1993 by Ian Chia. All rights reserved.

Driving rock feel.

2. The crippled man sat by the road and he cried ...
   Oh, show me the way ...
3. We all sat by the road and we cried ...
   Oh, show me the way ...
4. Jesus stood by the road and he cried ...
   Oh, I am the way, I am the truth, I am the life,
   The way to go home.
5. Jesus - (claps)
   Oh, I am the way ...

THE BLIND MAN

The blind man sat by the road
and he cried; 3 TIMES
Oh! show me the way; 3 TIMES
The way to go home.

The crippled man sat by the road
and he cried; 3 TIMES
Oh! show me the way; 3 TIMES
The way to go home.

We all sat by the road and we cried; 3 TIMES
Oh! show me the way; 3 TIMES
The way to go home.

Jesus stood by the road and he cried; 3 TIMES
Oh! I am the way, I am the truth,
I am the life,
The way to go home.

Jesus - CLAP ALONG TO THE BEAT
Oh, I am the way, I am the truth,
I am the life,
The way to go home.

Words and music: unknown.

The "Boom Boom" Song

Words and music: Grant Ward

With a lilt, swing eighths.

THE BOOM BOOM SONG

(Boom boom boom boom)
I was walking down the street
(Boom boom boom boom)
Just skipping to the beat
(Boom boom boom boom)
When a frown upon your face
My eyes did see.
(Wah wah wah wah
Boom boom boom boom)
Why you lookin' so sad?
(Boom boom boom boom)
When you ought to be glad!
(Boom boom boom boom)
'Cause Jesus gave his life for you and me.

Words and music: Grant Ward
© 1985 Chain Reaction Music

Can You Count the Stars?

Words and Music: Paul Field

2. Up in outer space, planets spinning round,
   Millions more than we can ever see.
   It's hard to understand, how God, who made it all,
   Still cares about someone like you and me.

CAN YOU COUNT THE STARS?

Can you count the stars shining in the sky?
Can you hold the moonlight in your hand?
Can you stop the waves
rolling on the shore?
Or find the place where rainbows
meet the land?

CHORUS
There is a Friend who knows
how all these things are done.
Jesus Lord of all, God's only Son.

Up in outer space, planets spinning round,
Millions more than we can ever see.
It's hard to understand,
how God, who made it all,
Still cares about someone
like you and me.

Words and music: Paul Field
© 1991 Daybreak Music Ltd

The Caterpillar Song

Words and music: Leigh Newton

THE CATERPILLAR SONG

The caterpillar died, the caterpillar died,
Oh, what a shame and everybody cried,
The caterpillar died, the caterpillar died,
Oh, how sad at Easter.

The butterfly was born,
The butterfly was born,
What a nice surprise, early Easter morn,
The butterfly was born,
The butterfly was born,
Oh, what joy at Easter.

Words and music: Leigh Newton
© 1986 Leigh Newton

Choosing Jesus

Words and music: Christine Williams
(c) Copyright 1985 by Christine Williams.

A Round.

♩ = 90 **Part One**

1. Ev - 'ry - one's spe - cial to Je - sus. He healed the sick not the heal - thy;
2. Choos - ing His way is not ea - sy; some - times it brings taunts and teas - ing.

He helped the poor not the weal - thy; Tur - ning the world up - side down.
He al - ways loves us and guides us, Je - sus will not let us down.

Part Two

Think like Je - sus, live like Je - sus,

love like Je - sus, Choos - ing Je - sus.

19

CHOOSING JESUS

Everyone's special to Jesus.
He healed the sick - not the healthy;
He helped the poor - not the wealthy;
Turning the world upside down

CHORUS
Think like Jesus, live like Jesus,
Love like Jesus, choosing Jesus.

Choosing his way is not easy;
Sometimes it brings taunts and teasing
He always loves us and guides us
Jesus will not let us down.

Words and music: Christine Williams
© 1985 Christine Williams

Don't Let the Devil Take the Truth Away

Words and Music: Angela Reith

2. There's a million tricks that the devil tries
   To stop the seed from growing and to make it die.
   He'll turn your friends against you,
   They will laugh and tease,
   Tell you it's too hard to do what Jesus says:
   CHORUS

3. He'll say you can be happy if you have great wealth,
   He'll tell you that the best way is to think of yourself
   Don't believe his lies and don't you listen to his talk
   Jesus is the one who knows the way to walk:
   CHORUS

DON'T LET THE DEVIL TAKE THE TRUTH

Jesus told a story, he said, listen here
My words are like the seeds
that are sown each year
He said, listen very carefully
so the seeds can rise
Don't you be distracted by the devil's lies:

CHORUS
Let the truth inside your soul
Let the truth make you whole
'Cos Jesus is the life
and Jesus has the last say
Don't let the devil take the truth away! TWICE

There's a million tricks that the devil tries
To stop the seed from growing
and to make it die
He'll turn your friends against you,
they will laugh and tease
Tell you it's too hard to do what Jesus
says:

CONTINUED ...

DON'T LET THE DEVIL TAKE THE TRUTH
CONTINUED

He'll say you can be happy
if you have great wealth
He'll tell you that the best way
is to think of yourself
Don't believe his lies and don't you listen
to his talk
Jesus is the one who knows
the way to walk:

CHORUS
Let the truth inside your soul
Let the truth make you whole
'Cos Jesus is the life
and Jesus has the last say
Don't let the devil take the truth away! TWICE

Words and music: Angela Reith
© 1985 Angela Reith

Driftin' Away

Words and music: David MacGregor

With a bounce, swing eights.

Drift - tin' a - way from each o - ther, it does no - one no good. And drift - tin' a - way from You, Je - sus; things don't turn out like they should. But Je - sus, You came ____ to help us. To get us back to - ge - ther a - gain; So may ev' - ry - one, ev' - ry - where know You, as a real for - giv - ing friend; a real for - giv - ing friend.

DRIFTIN' AWAY

**Driftin' away from each other
It does no one no good
And driftin' away from you, Jesus
things don't turn out like they should.
But Jesus, you came to help us
to get us back together again,
So may everyone, everywhere know you
As a real forgiving Friend,
A real forgiving Friend!**

Words and music: David MacGregor
© 1978 David MacGregor

Footsteps

Words and music: David MacGregor

26

FOOTSTEPS

CHORUS

I keep seein' footsteps
Jesus movin' over the land.
I keep hearin' them sayin'
Follow me, come take my hand
Come follow me, come take my hand.

VERSE

Follow me, high and low
Through ups and downs
Wherever you go.
Come on, and make those footsteps show!
I'll lead the way, you know. Oh ...CHORUS

Words and music: David MacGregor
© 1979 David MacGregor

Get Up!

Words and music: Chris Powell and K. Wood
(c) Copyright 1985 by C. Powell and K. Wood
All rights reserved.

CHORUS
2. Jesus showed us that He can make us new
   Get out of bed and ask Him what to do.
CHORUS
3. Jesus loves us all just like He said,
   Get out of bed and shake your sleepy head.

GET UP!

CHORUS

Get up out of bed
Have a yawn and scratch your head
And say 'Thank you, it's a brand new day.'
Stretch out, touch your toes
Blink your eyes and blow your nose
And say 'Thank you, it's a brand new day.'

Jesus taught us all to go his way
Get out of bed and go with him today.

Jesus showed us that he can make us new,
Get out of bed and ask him what to do.

Jesus loves us all just like he said,
Get out of bed and shake your sleepy head.

CODA

'Thank you, it's a brand new,
Thank you, it's a brand new,
Thank you, it's a brand new day!'

Words and music: C Powell and K Wood
© 1985 Complete Cukoo Music

Give Thanks to the Lord

Words and music: Janet Morgan

2. When you eat your dinner
   And you're all full up.
   And your mum says (name)
   Will you help wash up?

3. When you stretch up high
   And you touch the ground.
   When you stretch out wide
   And you turn around.

4. When you click your fingers
   And you stamp your feet.
   When you clap your hands
   And you slap your knees.

GIVE THANKS TO THE LORD

CHORUS

Give thanks to the Lord for he is good.
Give thanks to the Lord forever.
Give thanks to the Lord for he is good

When you jump out of bed
and you touch your toes,
When you brush your teeth
and put on your clothes.

When you eat your dinner
And you're all full up.
When your mum says ' YOUR NAME
Will you help wash up?'

When you stretch up high
And you touch the ground.
When you stretch out wide
And you turn around.

When you click your fingers
And you stamp your feet.
When you clap your hands
And you slap your knees.

CODA

Give thanks to the Lord. Amen!

Words and music: Janet Morgan
© 1989 Sea Dream Music

God Is Love

Words and music: Ross Langmead

GOD IS LOVE

God is love and love is giving
God gives me the life I have
The life I have leads me to singing
Sing that God is love.

Words and music: Ross Langmead

God Loves You Just the Way You Are

Words and music: Merrill Corney

GOD LOVES YOU JUST THE WAY YOU ARE

God loves you just the way you are.
God loves you just the way you are.
He made you that way
and he's with you night and day;
God loves you just the way you are.

God loves me just the way I am.
God loves me just the way I am.
He made me that way,
and he's with me night and day;
God loves me just the way I am.

Words and music: Merrill Corney
© 1985 Merrill Corney

God Made Caterpillars

Words and music: Jennie Flack
(c) Copyright 1983 by Just Life (Australia).

GOD MADE CATERPILLARS

A fat fluffy caterpillar sitting on my mat,
Wearing forty yellow gumboots
and a green and purple hat.
I poked him with my finger
and I flicked him with my toe,
But he positively, absolutely would not go.

God made caterpillars,
God made mountains,
God made kookaburras, God made the sea.
God made every single thing
in the whole world,
And God wants especially
to be friends with me.

God made caterpillars,
God made mountains
God made kookaburras, God made the sea.
Isn't it great that the God
who made everything,
Wants to be especially friends with me.

Words and music: Jennie Flack
© 1983 Just Life (Aust.)

God Made the World

Words unknown. Music: Heather Gwilliam.
(c) Copyright 1979 by Heather Gwilliam.

Fast and bluesy.
Swung eighths.

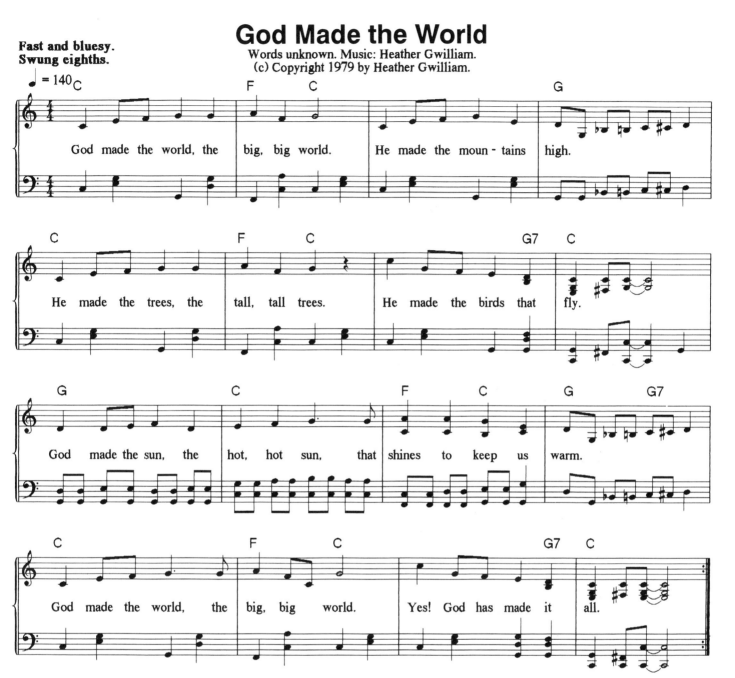

GOD MADE THE WORLD

God made the world,
the BIG, BIG world
He made the mountains high,
He made the trees,
the tall, tall trees,
He made the birds that fly.
God made the sun,
the hot, hot sun,
that shines to keep us warm.
God made the world,
the BIG, BIG world,
Yes! God has made it all!

Words: unknown
Music: Heather Gwilliam
© 1978 Heather Gwilliam

God with a Loving Heart

Words and music: Gill Hutchinson

2. He is the God who shows he cares,
He is the one who's always there,
He is the God with a loving heart.

He is the God whose praise we sing,
He is the Lord of everything.
He is the God with a loving heart.
He is the God with a loving heart.

GOD WITH A LOVING HEART

God of the earth and sky and sea,
great is his love for you and me,
He is the God - with a loving heart.

He is the God whose word is true,
He knows the things we say and do,
He is the God with a loving heart.
He wants us all to trust him
Our maker and our friend,
He's always there beside us,
His love will never end.

He is the God who shows he cares,
He is the one who's always there,
He is the God with a loving heart.

He is the God whose praise we sing,
He is the Lord of everything,
He is the God with a loving heart,
He is the God with a loving heart.

Words and music: Gill Hutchinson
© 1993 Sea Dream Music

Good Fri, Good Fri, Good Friday

Words and music: Gerry Holmes
(c) Copyright 1990 by Gerry Holmes. All rights reserved.

2. When his friends all turned and ran away,
   The soldiers nailed his hands and feet.
   On a lonely hill on a lonely day,
   Jesus died for you and me.
   CHORUS: On a Good Fri, Good Fri, Good Friday ...

3. When there's hat parades and Easter eggs
   And hot cross buns are in the stores
   We remember Jesus on the cross
   We remember who he suffered for.
   CHORUS: Remember Good Fri, Good Fri, Good Friday ...

41

GOOD FRI, GOOD FRI, GOOD FRIDAY

When the sky turned black and Jesus cried
That was a kind of victory
When the temple curtain was ripped apart
That was a sign for you and me.

CHORUS
It was a Good Fri, Good Fri, Good Friday
It was a Good Fri, Good Friday!
REPEAT

When his friends all turned and ran away
The soldiers nailed his hands and feet
On a lonely hill on a lonely day
Jesus died for you and me.

When there's hat parades and Easter eggs
And hot cross buns are in the stores
We remember Jesus on the cross
We remember who he suffered for.

Words and music: Gerry Holmes
© 1990 Gerry Holmes.

He Gets Things Done

Words and music: Robin Mann
(c) Copyright 1986 by Robin Mann. All rights reserved.

Gentle ballad

2. Lots of people make a big noise,
   Telling everybody of their deeds,
   God is different, very quiet,
   While he gives us what we really need.

3. With a baby in a cowshed,
   With a poor man hanging on a cross,
   He invites us, he receives us,
   He comes looking for us when we're lost.

HE GETS THINGS DONE

Like a seed that's growing secret
in the darkness of the underground,
no-one knows it, no-one sees it,
no-one hears it growing, not a sound.

CHORUS
He gets things done,
With a minimum of fuss,
he gets things done.
You may never hear the beating of his
drum
but that's the way the world is run.

Lots of people make a big noise
telling everybody of their deeds.
God is different, very quiet,
while he gives us what we really need.

With a baby in a cowshed,
with a poor man hanging on a cross
He invites us, he receives us,
he comes looking for us when we're lost.

Words and music: Robin Mann
© 1986 Robin Mann

The Helping Song

Words and music: Digby Hannah

Energetically.

♩. = 58

1. There once was a man as mean as could be. If he could take two then he'd try to take three. Then one day he took Je - sus for tea. Je - sus helped him to change. Well (Chorus) Je - sus helps mean - ies and good - ies and badd - ies. Je - sus helps laz - ies and happ - ies and sadd - ies. Je - sus helps lone - lies and mums, kids and dadd - ies and Je - sus wants us to help too.

2. Blind Bartimaeus, as all will agree
   Was wise to keep shouting as loud as could be,
   "Oh, please, Son of David, have mercy on me!"
   Jesus opened his eyes.
   CHORUS

3. Said Martha: "It's really my right to protest,
   I'm working so hard here while Mary just rests."
   Jesus replied, "Mary's chosen the best.
   Martha, come talk to me too."
   CHORUS

4. Once a poor lady, whom no-one could bear,
   Cried as she wiped Jesus' feet with her hair.
   She had found someone she knew really cared:
   Jesus made her so glad.
   CHORUS

45

THE HELPING SONG

There once was a man as mean as could be,
If he could take two
then he'd try to take three,
Then one day he took Jesus for tea,
Jesus helped him to change.

CHORUS
Well Jesus helps meanies and goodies
and baddies
Jesus helps lazies and happies and
saddies
Jesus helps lonelies
and mums, kids and daddies
And Jesus wants us to help too.

Blind Bartimaeus, as all will agree,
Was wise to keep shouting
as loud as could be,
'Oh, please, son of David,
have mercy on me!'
Jesus opened his eyes.

THE HELPING SONG CONTINUED

Said Martha: 'It's really my right to protest,
I'm working so hard here
while Mary just rests.'
Jesus replied,'Mary's chosen the best.
Martha, come talk to me too.'

CHORUS
Well Jesus helps meanies and goodies
and baddies
Jesus helps lazies and happies and
saddies
Jesus helps lonelies
and mums, kids and daddies
And Jesus wants us to help too.

Once a poor lady, whom no-one could bear
Cried as she wiped Jesus' feet with her hair
She had found someone
she knew really cared:
Jesus made her so glad.

Words and music: Digby Hannah
© 1981 Digby Hannah

How Much Am I Worth?

Words and music: Colin Gibson
(c) Copyright 1988 by C.A. Gibson. All rights reserved.

2. I am that bird that dropped to the ground,
The tiniest bird of them all,
And nobody knew, and nobody cared,
But the Father, who cares for us all.

3. I am that stone that fell from a ring,
That was precious beyond all compare;
And they hunted the house, till they cried out with joy,
When they saw it, still gleaming, down there.

4. I am that child who felt lost and afraid,
When she saw just how far she had roamed;
But they scoured the hills till they found her again,
And, rejoicing, they brought her safe home.

5. How much am I worth? Do I matter at all?
When I'm thinking it through may I see
That I'm worth all the love of the Son of God,
Who laid down his life just for me.

HOW MUCH AM I WORTH?

How much am I worth?
What value's in me?
Do I count, if I stand or I fall?
If I'm weak or I'm strong, if I win or I lose,
am I someone or no one at all?

CHORUS
I am worth everything,
everything, everything,
I am worth everything in the eyes of God;
REPEAT

I am that bird that dropped to the ground,
the tiniest bird of them all,
and nobody knew, and nobody cared,
but the Father, who cares for us all.

I am that stone that fell from a ring,
that was precious beyond all compare;
and they hunted the house,
till they cried out with joy
when they saw it, still gleaming, down
there.

CONTINUED

HOW MUCH AM I WORTH? CONTINUED

I am that child who felt lost and afraid,
when she saw just how far she had
roamed;
but they scoured the hills
till they found her again,
and, rejoicing, they brought her safe home.

CHORUS
I am worth everything,
everything, everything,
I am worth everything in the eyes of God.

REPEAT

How much am I worth?
Do I matter at all?
When I'm thinking it through may I see
that I'm worth all the love of the Son of
God,
who laid down his life just for me.

Words and music: Colin Gibson
© 1986 Colin Gibson

If You're Black or If You're White

Composer Unknown.

IF YOU'RE BLACK OR IF YOU'RE WHITE

If you're black or if you're white
or if you're in between,
God loves you!
If you're short or if you're tall
or if you're fat or lean,
God loves you!
He loves you when you're happy,
He loves you when you're sad...
He loves you when you're very good
and when you're very bad!

No matter what you look like
no matter what you do ...
God loves you!
Oh hallelujah!
God loves you!
Oh sock it to ya,
God loves you!
Shoo-by, doo-by, doo-by doo .. Doo-wah ..!!

Words and music: unknown

I Have a Name

Words and music: Robert Smith

2. I have a name and it's mine to keep,
   When I'm awake and when I'm asleep.
   God is a Father who knows me by name,
   His love is always the same.

3. I have a name and you have one too,
   We can be friends, just me and you.
   For every day we are learning to love
   Thanks to the Father above.

I HAVE A NAME

I have a name and my name means me.
I am a part of a family.
I have a name that they call me at home.
This name is my very own.

I have a name and it's mine to keep
When I'm awake
and when I'm asleep
God is a Father who knows me by name
His love is always the same.

All over the world you know
There's not another you
And God has made us to learn to care
Given each one of us love to share.

I have a name and you have one too
We can be friends, just me and you
For every day we are learning to love
Thanks to the Father above.

Words and music: Robert Smith

Image of God

Words and music: John Hardwick

2. Look at the wheel, it's a simple device,
   We use them on trains and cars and bikes.
   How on earth did we invent that?
   'Cause we're made in the image of God.

3. Monkeys are clever swinging in the trees,
   But how many monkeys know their ABC's?
   We're special without a doubt,
   'Cause we're made in the image of God.

IMAGE OF GOD

CHORUS
We can think things through,
we can work things out,
we can talk to each other,
we can sing and shout.
We know what's right
and we know what's wrong
'cause we're made in the image of God.
VERSES
See the clown juggling so high,
see the flying trapeze
flying through the sky.
How on earth can they do that?
'Cause we're made in the image of God!

Look at the wheel,
it's a simple device,
We use them on trains and cars and bikes.
How on earth did we invent that?
'Cause we're made in the image of God.

Monkeys are clever
swinging in the trees,
But how many monkeys know their ABC's?
We're special without a doubt,
'Cause we're made in the image of God.

Words and music: John Hardwick
© 1993 Daybreak Music

I Need a Friend

Words and music: Mandy Dyson

From "Faith is Like a Muscle". Published by Me'n'You Music.

2. When the other kids ruin everything you planned,
   You didn't start the fight
   But the teacher can't understand.
   When nobody wants to be your special friend,
   Say Jesus, Jesus.
CHORUS

I NEED A FRIEND

CHORUS
I need a friend, I need a friend,
when the night is dark
and the world's frightening.
I need a friend, I need a friend,
Lord Jesus won't you be my friend.

When all your friends tease,
and your Mum gets cross,
you can't do that maths
and the footy team lost.
When the cheat comes top
and doesn't get caught,
say Jesus, Jesus.

When the other kids ruin
everything you planned,
You didn't start the fight
but the teacher can't understand.
When nobody wants to be your special
friend, say Jesus, Jesus.

Words and music: Mandy Dyson
© 1985 Me'n'You Music

It's an Adventure

Words and music: Alan J. Price
(c) Copyright 1990 by Daybreak Music. All rights reserved.

With excitement.

IT'S AN ADVENTURE

It's an adventure, following Jesus.
It's an adventure learning of him.
It's an adventure, living for Jesus.
It's an adventure, following him.

Let's go where he leads us,
turn away from wrong;
for we know we can trust him
to help us as we go along.

It's an adventure, following Jesus.
It's an adventure, learning of him.
It's an adventure, living for Jesus.
It's an adventure, following him.

Words and music: Alan J Price
© 1990 Daybreak Music

I've Never Seen an Elephant

Words and music: Colin Gibson

Jauntily.

I've ne-ver seen an e-le-phant, and an e-le-phant's ne-ver seen me.

I can't swing like a mon-key can from the branch of a tro-pi-cal tree.

I don't roar like a li-on does, but a li-on can't read my books.

I'm not as huge as a hip-po is, but a hip-po has-n't my looks.

Thank you God, thank you God, for it's ve-ry plain to see that the

an-i-mals like the way they are, and I'm glad that I'm like me.

I'VE NEVER SEEN AN ELEPHANT

I've never seen an elephant,
and an elephant's never seen me.
I can't swing like a monkey can
from the branch of a tropical tree.
I don't roar like a lion does,
but a lion can't read my books.
I'm not as huge as a hippo is,
but a hippo hasn't my looks.
Thank you God, thank you God,
for it's very plain to see
that the animals like the way they are,
and I'm glad that I'm like me.

Words and music: Colin Gibson
© 1988 Colin Gibson

Jesus Came

Words: Christine Williams Music: Traditional
(c) Copyright 1985 by C. Williams. All rights reserved.

2. And he told the sick man to leave his bed,
   Blind eyes he made see.
   He healed the deaf and he raised the dead,
   His word was victory.

3. But we can't love Jesus just as we should,
   Often we disobey.
   And Jesus who died to make us good
   Forgives us as we pray.

JESUS CAME

CHORUS

Jesus came to show us that God loves us so,
loves us so, loves us so.
Jesus came to show us that God loves us so,
and that we can love him too.

And he gave us stories that make us see,
pictures to help us know,
that we can be in his family
because God loves us so.

And he told the sick man to leave his bed,
Blind eyes he made see.
He healed the deaf and he raised the dead.
His word was victory.

But we can't love Jesus just as we should.
Often we disobey.
And Jesus who died to make us good
forgives us as we pray.

Words and music: Christine Williams
© 1985 Christine Williams

Jesus is Greater

Words and music: Gill Hutchinson

Upbeat rock.

JESUS IS GREATER

Jesus is greater than the greatest heroes.
Jesus is closer than the closest friends.
He came down from heaven
and he died to save us,
to show us love that never ends.   REPEAT

Son of God, King of earth and heaven.
He's the light,
follow in his way.
He's the truth,
that we can believe in,
and he's the life, he's living today.   REPEAT

Words and music: Gill Hutchinson
© 1992 Sea Dream Music

Jesus is the Best Friend

Music: Traditional   Words: Merrill Corney

Je - sus is the best friend, the best friend, the best friend.

Je - sus is the best friend, the best friend of all.

Je - sus is the best friend, the best friend, the best friend.

Je - sus is the best friend, the best friend of all.

JESUS IS THE BEST FRIEND

Jesus is the best friend,
the best friend,
the best friend.

Jesus is the best friend,
the best friend of all.
Jesus is the best friend
the best friend, the best friend.
Jesus is the best friend,
the best friend of all.

Words: Merrill Corney
Music: Traditional
© 1985 Merrill Corney

Jesus Loves the Boys and Girls

Copyright unknown. Arrangement by Ian Chia.

Brightly.

♩ = 140

JESUS LOVES THE BOYS AND GIRLS

Jesus loves the boys and girls
like me, me, me.
Jesus loves the boys and girls
like me, me, me.
Boys and girls like me
sat upon his knee;
Jesus loves the boys and girls
like me, me, me.

Words and music: unknown

Light of the World

Words and music: Jennie Flack
(c) Copyright 1986 by Just Life (Australia).

Brightly, swing eighths.

♩ = 132

Je-sus said, some-thing won-der-ful, Je-sus said, some-thing true.

What he said, you should lis-ten to 'cause what he said was meant for you.

I am the Light of the World, don't live in dark-ness.

I am the Light of the World, come fol-low me.

I am the Light of the World, do what I tell you. and to-

ge-ther we'll live, to-ge-ther we'll live, to-ge-ther we'll live, to-ge-ther we'll live,

the right way.

LIGHT OF THE WORLD

Jesus said, something wonderful,
Jesus said, something true.
What he said, you should listen to
'cause what he said was meant for you.

I am the Light of the World,
don't live in darkness.
I am the Light of the World,
come follow me.
I am the Light of the World,
do what I tell you.
And together we'll live,
together we'll live   THREE TIMES
the right way.

Words and music: Jennie Flack
© 1986 Just Life (Australia)

Mighty God

Words and music: Gerry Holmes.

MIGHTY GOD

He's a mighty God and he's mighty strong.
He can change the world,
even beat King Kong.
And he cares for us in so many ways
if we trust in him, we will grow and change.

Stronger than any man,
even more than Superman,
Bad guys run and hide
when they see he's on our side.

Words and music: Gerry Holmes
© 1992 Gerry Holmes

Millions of People

Words: Ralph Chambers Music: Paul Field
(c) Copyright 1991 Daybreak Music Ltd.

Gently.

♩ = 110

1. In this world there are mil - lions of peo - ple. Peo - ple just like you and me.
2. In this world there are mil - lions of prob - lems. Prob - lems for us all to see.

Black and white, hap - py, sad, rich and poor, good or bad.
Pride and en - vy, bit - ter - ness, hate and greed, self - ish - ness.

But God loves ev - 'ry - one, and God loves me.
But God solves prob - lems and God helps me.

75

MILLIONS OF PEOPLE

In this world there are millions of people.
People just like you and me.
Black and white,
happy, sad, rich and poor,
good or bad.
But God loves every one,
and God loves me.

In this world there are millions of
problems.
Problems for us all to see.
Pride and envy,
bitterness, hate, greed, selfishness.
But God solves problems
and God helps me.

Words: Ralph Chambers
Music: Paul Field
© 1991 Daybreak Music Ltd

Mystery World

Words and music: Angela Reith

2. It's a mystery world but you understand the puzzle,
'Cos you came into the muddle of our myst'ry world.
It's a mystery world but you promise to be with us,
Making sense of all the chaos in our mystery world.

MYSTERY WORLD

It's a mystery world,
we don't understand the sadness.
And we want to see more gladness,
in our mystery world.
It's a mystery world,
and we need a lot of guiding,
for the truth seems to be hiding,
behind closed doors.

CHORUS
So Jesus open our eyes to see
that you can open up every door,
that you can do a whole lot more
than we believed before.
So Jesus open our eyes to see
that you can open up every door,
that you can do a whole lot more
than we believed.

CONTINUED ...

MYSTERY WORLD   CONTINUED

It's a mystery world
but you understand the puzzle,
'Cause you came into the muddle
of our mystery world.
It's a mystery world
but you promise to be with us,
making sense of all the chaos
in our mystery world.

CHORUS
So Jesus open our eyes to see
that you can open up every door,
that you can do a whole lot more
than we believed before.
So Jesus open our eyes to see
that you can open up every door,
that you can do a whole lot more
than we believed.

Words and music: Angela Reith
© 1985 Angela Reith

No Mountain High Enough

Words and music: Charles Kirby

NOTE: An OHP master is not available for this song. See page 113.

2. No king is great enough, no army large enough,
No power strong enough to hide me from God's love.

3. No sin is bad enough, no troubles tough enough,
No questions hard enough to hide me from God's love.

1,2,3, Follow Me

Words and music: Derek Llewellyn & Janet Morgan

Jauntily

2. Two sons of Zebedee, James and John;
   Sitting in their boat so calm.
   One day Jesus came to visit and said:
   "Stop what you're doing and follow me."

3. Three in a family, so much to do,
   Mary, Martha, Lazarus too;
   One day Jesus came to visit and said:
   "Stop what you're doing and follow me."

4. Millions of families everyday,
   At home, at work, at school and play;
   One day Jesus says to everyone:
   "Stop what you're doing and follow me."

123 FOLLOW ME

One man was Peter, he lived by the sea,
a fisherman by trade was he;
One day Jesus came to visit and said:
'Stop what you're doing and follow me.'

'Follow me, follow me; just
stop what you're doing and follow me.' REPEAT

Two sons of Zebedee, James and John,
sitting in their boat so calm;
One day Jesus came to visit and said:
'Stop what you're doing and follow me.'

Three in a family, so much to de,
Mary, Martha, Lazarus too:
One day Jesus came to visit and said:
'Stop what you're doing and follow me.'

Millions of families everyday,
at home, at work, at school and play;
One day Jesus says to everyone:
'Stop what you're doing and follow me.'

Words and music: Derek Llewellyn and Janet Morgan
© 1988 Sea Dream Music

Only Jesus

Words: Ralph Chambers Music: Paul Field

Jauntily.

ONLY JESUS

You can't catch a plane
to take you to heaven.
Not even a space ship can get that far.
You can't take a hovercraft
or helicopter journey
or drive in the fastest racing car.
Only Jesus, only Jesus,
only Jesus is the way.
Only Jesus, only Jesus,
only Jesus is the way.

Words and music: Paul Field
© 1991 Daybreak Music Ltd.

Our God is So Big

Composer Unknown
Arrangement by Ian Chia.

OUR GOD IS SO BIG

Our God is so big,
so strong and so mighty,
there's nothing our God cannot do!

REPEAT

The mountains are his,
the rivers are his,
the whole world is under his smile.
Our God is so big,
so strong and so mighty,
there's nothing our God cannot do!

Words and music: Composer and copyright owner unknown

The Road Sign Song

(or "This is the Wrong Way")

Words and music: Gary & Christine Nelson

THE ROAD SIGN SONG

This is the wrong way,
turn back, follow Jesus.
There's only one way,
this is the track, follow Jesus.
Stop, look and listen
to what God has to say.

There's only one way,
this is the track, follow Jesus.
If we choose our own way,
heading where we please,
there'll be a dead end, around the bend.

Follow Jesus.
Give way to Jesus.
Let him take control.
He'll be your strong friend,
right to the end.
Follow Jesus.

Words and music: Gary and Christine Nelson
© 1990 G & C Nelson

Sandy Lands

Words and music: Karen Lafferty
(c) Copyright 1981 by Maranatha! Music.

2. Some people live just the way they want;
Following the crowd next door.
They don't know a better way,
Feelings change from day to day,
And they're slipping on the sandy shore.

3. Christ is the rock where it's best to build,
He tells us how to live;
For his word contains the plans,
And his spirit helps our hands,
Try the sure foundation Jesus is.

SANDY LANDS

Don't build your house on the sandy land;
Don't build it too near the shore.
Well it might be kind of nice,
but you'll have to build it twice,
Oh, you'll have to build your house
once more.

CHORUS
You'd better build your house on the rock.
Make a firm foundation on the solid rock.
Well the storms may come and go,
but the peace of God you will know.

Some people live just the way they want;
following the crowd next door.
They don't know a better way,
feelings change from day to day,
and they're slipping on the sandy shore.

CONTINUED ...

SANDY LANDS CONTINUED

Christ is the Rock where it's best to build.
He tells us how to live.
For his word contains the plans,
and his Spirit helps our hands.
Try the sure foundation Jesus is.

CHORUS
You'd better build your house on the rock.
Make a firm foundation on the solid rock.
Well the storms may come and go,
but the peace of God you will know.

Words and music: Karen Lafferty
Words verses 2 and 3: Felicia Edgecombe
© 1981 Maranatha! Music

See the Little Seed

Words and music: John McRae

Freely to match actions.

See the lit-tle seed, ly-ing on the ground. God does some-thing won-der-ful to ev-'ry seed I've found. He makes them grow, grow, grow, grow!

See the lit-tle boy, stand-ing on the ground. God does some-thing won-der-ful to ev-'ry boy I've found. He makes them grow, grow, grow, grow!

See the lit-tle girl, stand-ing on the ground. God does some-thing won-der-ful to ev-'ry girl I've found. He makes them grow, grow, grow, grow! Grow.

SEE THE LITTLE SEED

See the little seed,
lying on the ground.
God does something wonderful
to every seed I've found
He makes them grow, grow, grow, grow!

See the little boy,
standing on the ground.
God does something wonderful
to every boy I've found.
He makes them grow, grow, grow, grow!

See the little girl
standing on the ground.
God does something wonderful
to every girl I've found.
He makes them grow, grow, grow, grow!
Grow!

Words and music: John McRae
© 1981 John McRae

Sorrowing Song

Words and music: Robin Mann

2. Children are crying, hungry for food.
   Sick from disease - God, are you good?
   People are homeless, lost and alone:
   God, are you hiding? Where have you gone?

3. Why do the rich ones steal from the poor?
   Why do they build their weapons of war?
   How can you stand the torture and pain,
   Hope disappearing, freedom in chains?

4. Jesus, remind us that you are found
   With those who cry, with those who are bound;
   Where there is suffering, you will be there -
   Help us to follow, Lord, hear our prayer.

94

SORROWING SONG

Lord, hear my praying,
listen to me;
you know there's evil in what I see.
I know I am part of all that is wrong.
Still won't you hear my sorrowing song.

Children are crying, hungry for food;
sick from diseases - God, are you good?
People are homeless, lost and alone:
God are you hiding?
Where have you gone?

Why do the rich ones steal from the poor?
Why do they build their weapons of war?
How can you stand the torture and pain,
hope disappearing, freedom in chains?

Jesus, remind us that you are found
with those who cry,
with those who are bound;
where there is suffering, you will be there -
help us to follow, Lord, hear our prayer.

Words and music: Robin Mann
© 1986 Robin Mann

Special

Words and music: Paul Field

96

SPECIAL

There is no-one else like you,
there's no-one else like me.
Each of us is special to God,
that's the way it's meant to be.
I'm special, you're special,
we're special don't you see?

There is no-one else like you.
there's no-one else like me.
Black or white, short or tall,
good or bad, God loves us all.
Loud or quiet, fat or thin,
each of us is special to him.

Words and music: Paul Field
© 1991 Daybreak Music Ltd.

Stop Still and Listen

Words and music: Digby Hannah

2. Listen to the owl, listen to the owl.
Lying in the night thinking "Who's out there?"
There's the hoot of an owl in the night somewhere,
It's good to know we're safely in God's care.

3. Listen to the wind, listen to the wind.
It whispers, it rustles, it howls and it whines.
Where it goes, who can find?
Let's listen for the wind of God stirring in our mind.

STOP STILL AND LISTEN

CHORUS

The sounds in God's world all agree,
he made it up so beautif'ly.
More there is to hear when we ...
Stop still and listen very carefully.

Listen to the surf, listen to the surf,
The breakers crash while the sea swell
bends.
Some of God's big things
never seem to end.
How great that the maker of the sea
wants to be our friend.

Listen to the owl. listen to the owl.
Lying in the night thinking:
'Who's out there?'
There's the hoot of an owl
in the night somewhere.
It's good to know we're
safely in God's care.

Listen to the wind,
listen to the wind.
It whispers, it rustles,
it howls and it whines.
Where it goes, who can find?
Let's listen for the wind
of God stirring in our mind.

Words and music: Digby Hannah
© 1982 Digby Hannah

Thank You For the Friends

Words and music: Leigh Newton
(c) Copyright 1989 by Leigh Newton. All rights reserved.

100

THANK YOU FOR THE FRIENDS

Thank you for the friends and family.
Thank you for the earth and the salty sea;
for plants that clean the air
and creatures everywhere.
And thank you God for me.

Words and music: Leigh Newton
© 1989 Leigh Newton

This is God's World

Words: Ralph Chambers Music: Paul Field

THIS IS GOD'S WORLD

Don't know much about the ozone layer.
Rain forests seem miles away.
But each of us can be a player,
fight to save the world God has made.

This is God's world.
This is God's world,
and you're a member of the human race..
This is God's world.
This is God's world.
Let's try to make it a better place.

Words and music: Ralph Chambers and Paul Field
©1991 Daybreak Music Ltd

Together

Words and music: Jan Taylor
From the musical "Hercules and other songs"

TOGETHER

**Together, together,
together we make a great team.
Together, together,
together we make a great team.**

**Working together, playing together,
laughing together, praying together,
Helping together, singing together.
Together we make a great team.**

Words and music: Jan Taylor
© 1987 Jan Taylor

Where Do All the Good Things Come From?

Words and music: Marion Lemin
(c) Copyright 1981 by M.D. Lemin. All rights reserved.

Fast shuffle.
♩ = 152

1. Did you ev-er see a kook-a-bur-ra laugh? Did you ev-er see a gir-

raffe? Did you ev-er ride in on a wave? Did you ev-er see a pup-py act

brave? Where do all the good things (Chorus) come from? Good things great and

small. Where do all the good things come from? God made them all.

2. Did you ever keep a cocoon?
Did you ever see a full moon?
Did you ever hold a fluffy new chick?
Did you ever see a clown do tricks?

3. Have you ever been in a fight?
And maybe cried all the night?
Did you make up and become friends?
Ain't it good how the broken things mend?

WHERE DO ALL THE GOOD THINGS COME FROM?

Did you ever see a kookaburra laugh?
Did you ever see a giraffe?
Did you ever ride in on a wave?
Did you ever see a puppy act brave?

CHORUS
Where do all the good things come from?
Good things great and small.
Where do all the good things come from?
God made them all

Did you ever keep a cocoon?
Did you ever see a full moon?
Did you ever hold a fluffy new chick?
Did you ever see a clown do tricks?

Have you ever been in a fight?
And maybe cried all the night?
Did you ever make up and become
friends?
Ain't it good how the broken things mend.

Wider Than the Universe

Words and music: Grant Ward

With confidence, swung eighths.

WIDER THAN THE UNIVERSE

Wider than the universe,
deeper than the sea.
Higher than a mountain,
taller than a tree.
I don't understand how it can be,
but oh! how great God's love for me!

Words and music: Grant Ward
© 1985 Chain Reaction Music

Yes, God is Bigger Than I Am

Words and Music: L. Mayfield, E. Lippy

Gently.

Lyrics:

Yes, God is big-ger than I am, strong-est of all; He's the migh-ty cre-a-tor yet He hears when I call. He con-trols all that hap-pens, His pow'r is plain to see. And I know that He loves me, for with His pow'r He cares for me.

110

YES, GOD IS BIGGER THAN I AM

Yes, God is bigger than I am,
strongest of all;
He's the mighty creator yet
he hears when I call.
He controls all that happens,
his power is plain to see.
And I know that he loves me,
for with his power he cares for me.

Words and music: L Mayfield and E Lippy (Revised)
© 1976/80 Child Evangelism Fellowship Inc.

SOURCES AND COPYRIGHT INFORMATION

Every effort has been made to provide here a complete listing of owners of copyright and current addresses. We apologise for any errors or omissions and will rectify any mistakes in future editions.

All day long
Paul Field © 1991 Daybreak Music Ltd
Silverdale Road, Eastbourne
East Sussex, BN20 7AB, England
Blind man
Composer and copyright owner unknown
Boom boom song
Grant J Ward © 1985 Chain Reaction Music
46 Ardyne Street, Murrumbeena
Victoria 3163, Australia
Can you count the stars?
Paul Field © 1991 Daybreak Music Ltd
Caterpillar song
© 1986 Leigh Newton,
31 Somerset Road, Aldgate
South Australia 5154, Australia
Choosing Jesus
© 1985 Christine Williams
2 Foxleigh, Billericay
Essex CM12 9NS, England
Don't let the devil take the truth away
© 1985 Angela Reith
47 Mayton Street
London N7 6QP, England
Driftin' away
© 1978 David McGregor
27 Harwood Street, North Rockhampton
Queensland 4701, Australia
Footsteps
© 1979 David McGregor
Get up
Chris Powell & K Wood
© 1983/85 Sea Dream Music
PO Box 13533, London E7 OSG, England
Give thanks to the Lord for he is good
Janet Morgan © 1989 Sea Dream Music
God is love
© 1981 Ross Langmead
62 Kernot Street, Spotswood
Victoria 3015, Australia
God loves you just the way you are
© 1985 Merrill Corney
27 King Street, Balwyn
Victoria 3103, Australia
God made caterpillars
Jennie Flack © 1983 Just Life Australia Pty Ltd
Agent: Willow Connection Pty Ltd
PO Box 288, Brookvale
New South Wales 2100, Australia

God made the world
© 1979 Heather Gwilliam
5 Panorama Crescent, Mt Riverview
New South Wales 2774, Australia
God with a loving heart
Gill Hutchinson © 1993 Sea Dream Music
Good Fri, Good Fri, Good Friday
© 1990 Gerry Holmes
Fusion Arts Colony, 'The Mansions'
Malmsbury, Victoria 3446, Australia
He gets things done
© 1986 Robin Mann
54 Currawong Crescent, Modbury Heights
South Australia 5092, Australia
Helping song
© 1981 Digby Hannah
49 Forrest Avenue, Newhaven
Victoria 3925, Australia
How much am I worth?
© 1988 Colin Gibson
28 Mitchell Avenue, Dunedin
New Zealand
If you're black or if you're white
Composer and copyright owner unknown
I have a name
© 1987 Robert Smith
119 Murchison Street, St Ives
New South Wales 2075, Australia
Image of God
John Hardwick © 1993 Daybreak Music Ltd
I need a friend
Mandy Dyson © 1985 Me'n'You Music
From 'Faith is like a muscle'
20 Cumming Street, Blackwood
South Australia 5051, Australia
It's an adventure
Alan J Price © 1990 Daybreak Music Ltd
I've never seen an elephant
© 1981 Colin Gibson
Jesus came
© 1985 Christine Williams
Jesus is greater
Gill Hutchinson © 1992 Sea Dream Music
Jesus is the best friend
© 1985 Merrill Corney
Jesus loves the boys and girls
Composer and copyright owner unknown
Light of the world
Jennie Flack © 1986 Just Life (Australia)

THEMATIC INDEX

Friendship
I need a friend
Thank you for the friends
Together

Following Jesus
It's an adventure
1, 2, 3 Follow me

Forgiveness
Driftin' away

God - his creation
God made caterpillars
God made the world
This is God's world
Where do all the good
   things come from?

his love
All day long
Can you count the stars?
God is love
God loves you just the way
   you are
God with a loving heart
How much am I worth?
I have a name
If you're black or if you're white
Mighty God
Millions of people
No mountain high enough
Special
Stop still and listen
Wider than the universe
Yes, God is bigger than I am

his power
Can you count the stars?
He gets things done
Mighty God
Our God is so big
Yes, God is bigger than I am

his style/nature
All day long
God with a loving heart
He gets things done

Growing
All day long
Image of God
See the little seed

Individual uniqueness
God loves you just
   the way you are
How much am I worth?
I have a name
Image of God
I've never seen an elephant
See the little seed
Special
Thank you for the friends

Jesus - calling followers
Choosing Jesus
Footsteps
It's an adventure
1, 2, 3 Follow me
The road sign song

Jesus - death and resurrection
Boom Boom Song
Caterpillar Song
Good Fri, Good Fri

forgiveness
Driftin' away
Jesus came

Friend
Footsteps
The helping song
I need a friend
Jesus is greater
Jesus is the best friend
Jesus loves the boys/girls

Healer
The blind man
Jesus came

parables
Don't let the Devil take
   the truth away
Sandy lands

Leader
Choosing Jesus
1, 2, 3 Follow me
The road sign song

Light
Light of the world

Saviour
Jesus is greater
Millions of people

Teacher
Get up!
Jesus came
Sandy lands

Way
The blind man
Only Jesus
The road sign song

Listening
Don't let the Devil take
   the truth away
Stop still and listen

New beginnings
Get up!

Obeying God's word
Don't let the Devil take
   the truth away
Jesus came
Light of the world

Prayer
Sorrowing song

Sin and temptation
Don't let the Devil take
   the truth away
Millions of people
Mystery world
Sorrowing Song

Thankfulness
Get up!
Give thanks to the Lord
God is love
Thank you for the friends

BIBLICAL INDEX

15:13	God is love
	Jesus is greater
20:24-30	Mystery world

Acts
16:14-15	He gets things done
16:16-40	Our God is so big
17:24	Millions of people

Romans
5:6-8	How much am I worth?
5:8	Boom Boom Song
5:10-11	Driftin' away
6:23	Only Jesus
8:18-22	This is God's world
8:31-39	Mighty God
	No mountain high enough
11:33-36	Yes God is bigger
12:10	Together

I Corinthians
15:3-6	Caterpillar Song
15:19-20	Boom Boom song

2 Corinthians
5:17-18	Choosing Jesus
5:20	Driftin' away

Ephesians
2:4	Yes God is bigger
3:21	Mystery world

Philippians
4:8-9	Choosing Jesus

1 Peter
3:18	Boom Boom song

2 Peter
1:5-8	Road sign song
	Together

Hebrews
1:1-3	Mystery world
12:2	It's an adventure

James
1:17	Thank you for the friends
	Where do all the good things come from?

1 John
4:4	Mighty God
4:9-11	Millions of people
4:19	God is love